chocolate

with Vimrod

chocolate

life is a struggle between good, evil, and chocolate

Vimrod by Lisa Swerling and Ralph Lazar

Andrews McMeel Publishing, LLC

Kansas City • Sydney • London

my new year's
resolution
is to start
thinking
about beginning
to consider
eating less
chocolate

i am a chocolate.

if you don't eat me now, **i will destroy you** and all that you stand for.

i spy with my little eye
something beginning
with **choc**
and ending with
lit

i only eat
free-range
chocolates

my favorite color is
chocolate

actually, forget the
mushrooms and anchovies.
if i could just have a

sprinkling of chocolate

on my pizza, that
would be great.

scientists
have created genetically modified sheep that poo chocolate.

i am going to get my shepherd's license.

if there were only **two** chocolate bars left on planet earth and they took refuge in your home, would you:

1. hand them over to the **government**?

2. let them **breed?**

3. **eat** them?

i don't love chocolate

i
love
chocolate<u>s</u>

i am **happy** because today i am going to eat one point three pounds of **chocolate**

are two of the UK's most familiar
graphic artists. Through their company,
Last Lemon, they have spawned a catwalk
of popular cartoon characters, which
includes Harold's Planet, The Brainwaves,
Blessthischick, and, of course, Vimrod.

Writers, artists, and designers, they are
married with two children, and spend
their time between London and various
beaches on the Indian Ocean.

- -

ISBN-13: 978-0-7407-7388-4
ISBN-10: 0-7407-7388-7

10 11 12 13 14 TEN 10 9 8 7 6 5 4 3 2 1

The authors assert the moral right to be identified as the authors of this work.

www.vimrod.com
www.andrewsmcmeel.com

ATTENTION: SCHOOLS AND BUSINESSES
Andrews McMeel books are available at quantity discounts with bulk
purchase for educational, business, or sales promotional use. For
information, please write to: Special Sales Department, Andrews McMeel
Publishing, LLC, 1130 Walnut Street, Kansas City, Missouri 64106.